# Jeff Koon
# Andy Powell

*Illustrated by*

# Tim Carroll

FREE PRESS
*New York London Toronto Sydney Singapore*

# Wearing of This Garment Does Not Enable You to Fly

101 Real Dumb Warning Labels

*f*P

FREE PRESS
A Division of Simon & Schuster Inc.
1230 Avenue of the Americas
New York, NY 10020

Copyright © 2003 by Jeff Koon and Andy Powell for text;
Tim Carroll for illustrations

FREE PRESS and colophon are
trademarks of Simon & Schuster, Inc.

For information about special discounts for bulk purchases,
please contact Simon & Schuster Special Sales:
1-800-456-6798 or business@simonandschuster.com

Designed by Bonni Leon-Berman

Manufactured in the United States of America

1  3  5  7  9  10  8  6  4  2

Library of Congress Cataloging-in-Publication data is available

ISBN 0-7432-4475-3

# Contents

# Preface

Some time ago a friend told me, "Stupid should hurt." I just laughed, but over the past year the truth of that statement has been made clearer to Jeff and me. Stupid actually does hurt, if the warnings we have collected have any reason to exist at all. Jeff and I found one warning on a car sunscreen—one of the large folding ones that cool your car in the summer: "Remove shade before operating vehicle." I've been guilty of driving in the winter with a bit of frost on my windshield, but *someone* must have decided to drive with the sunshade up, right? It is through the gratuitous mixture of stupidity and litigation that it has been possible for Jeff and me to present this collection, so give yourself a pat on the back if you've ever applied Preparation H internally, tried to dive in the 0' 0" section of your public swimming pool, or given ant poison to small children as a toy: you've helped further the career of two aspiring college freshmen.

Jeff and I take our responsibility as "exposers of the dumb" pretty seriously. We searched high and low shelves for these warnings. And we endured some adversity. As we walked through stores closely examining each and every product for dumb warnings, we became magnets for rent-a-cops. Of course, we are teenage guys, which seems invariably to arouse the suspicion of all security personnel in towns small and large. That was not the only peril of warning-shopping: there was always the looming risk of someone you know actually catching you in the act. "It's for my book" simply doesn't cut it when you're caught in a Wal-Mart holding a bag of adult diapers.

Fortunately Jeff and I are accustomed to being the subjects of ridiculous public spectacle. Following the success of our first book, *You May Not Tie an Alligator to a Fire Hydrant: 101 Real Dumb Laws*, we were invited to New York for a media tour, and our schedule included an unforgettable photo shoot with a magazine. We knew that the photographer wanted to get shots of us violating some laws—however, we didn't know this meant standing on the corner of Fifth Avenue and Broadway for three hours in a circa 1920 swimsuit while foreign tourists talked about "crazy Americans" as they passed. Even stranger, perhaps, was the photographer who tied Jeff and me to a fire hydrant, in my own neighborhood, for an hour and a half. To this day, I'm not sure the neighbors knew what was happening.

In looking over our collection of dumb warnings we can see certain types emerging. Certain products are intended to cure specific ailments or to be used for particular applications, but knowing what the product is really for and when to apply it is not always clear, as it seems, at least to some of us. One might assume that toilet cleaner should be applied to a dirty toilet. Apparently, though, a select group of people also think that toilet cleaner is good for baking, eye irritation, or as a sexual stimulant.

Manufacturers of products of all sorts seem to enjoy informing their customers of the most blatantly obvious information. Certainly, it fills up the package with more "interesting" content to read, but why not just cut to the chase and tell us what we really *need* to know?

There are various other loose categories, including "Don't eat it" and "If it's hot, it's hot," but we don't want to get too taxonomic about our warnings. Enjoy dipping into this book whenever life begins to seem safe and dull. But please note: this book does not enable you to fly—or do anything at all!

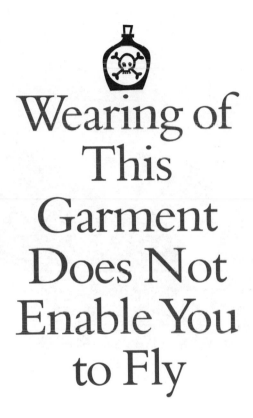

# Wearing of This Garment Does Not Enable You to Fly

### Spare Bladder

# Not suitable for human consumption.

This is a bag for urinating in while hunting in a tree stand. If you are in the habit of eating raw deer meat it might seem like a nice snack. . . .

**McDonald's Coffee Cup**

# Caution:
# HOT!

For this one we have to thank the famous suit against McDonald's for coffee that was too hot for at least one customer's lap.

**ChapStick Lip Moisturizer**

# Keep out
# of eyes.

**Boudreaux's Butt Paste**

# Avoid contact with eyes.

**Homelite Zip Start Vac
Attack Blower**

# Do not point blower in direction of people or pets.

Wild animals and leaves are presumably okay?

**Bono 527 Multi-Purpose Cement**

# Exposure may result in confusion.

Anyone who sniffs glue is more than confused.

**The Web Filter Fresh Air Freshener**

# Not for human consumption.

**3M Auto-Pak Aluminum Oxide
Automotive Sandpaper**

Safety information: Work
smart every time.
To change sheets,
wait until sander has
completely stopped.

**Bowl Fresh Automatic**
**(2-inch diameter toilet bowl cleaner tablets)**

# Harmful if swallowed.

We know a kid who can put a whole orange in his mouth—but that's beside the point.

**Munchkin First Aid Friends Reusable
Cold Pack for Bumps and Bruises**

# First Aid Friends
# are not a
# replacement
# for professional
# medical care.

**Bell Heavy Duty Integrated Cable Lock**

# Warning:
# Make sure lock does not interfere with safe operation of bicycle (braking, steering, etc.).

### Sun StarOffice End User License Agreement

# You acknowledge that software is not designed, licensed or intended for use in the design, construction, operation or maintenance of any nuclear facility. Sun disclaims any express or implied warranty of fitness for such uses.

Dr. Evil or other mad scientists seeking world domination, please note.

**20-inch Beach Ball**

# Caution: Not a life saving device.

**Super Bang Ring Caps**

# Never carry caps in pocket as caps may ignite and cause burn injuries.

At no time should anyone
be allowed
to lean or swing on
the oven door.
The oven is for food
preparation only.
It should not be used
to dry clothes or
newspapers.

**STP Power Steering Fluid**

# Do not swallow.

**Gummy Guard—The Candy Mouth Guard**

# FUN CANDY . . . NOT intended to protect you in contact sports.

**Panasonic Combi NE-C1153 Industrial Oven**

# Caution—Hot.
# Do not touch
# hot oven.

**Kellogg's Pop-Tarts Frosted Cherry**

# Caution:
# If pastry is overheated, frosting/filling can become extremely hot and could cause burns.

If it is extremely hot, it is extremely hot, right?

**Weber Genesis Silver C Gas Grill**

# Caution:
# Surface will
# be warm when
# in use.
# Do not use
# matches, lighters,
# or flame to check
# for leaks.

**Sunbeam Simple Press Iron**

# Warning:
# To prevent the risk of burns, keep your hand away from the area being steamed.

**Pressuremate CO$^2$ Cartridges—
Automatic Pressure for Gas Lanterns
and Stoves**

# Warning:
# Contents under pressure.

**Hungry Jack Lite Syrup**

# Caution: Syrup bottle may be hot.

After lengthy instructions on
how to heat the bottle.

**GE SmartWater Water Heater**

# Hotter water increases the risk of scald injury.

**Glade PlugIns**

# If the plug does not fit fully in the outlet, reverse the plug.

This is an air-freshening device—

maybe it makes you stupid, too.

**50 Water Bombs**
(water balloons)

# This bag is not a toy.

Yes indeed, it's the real thing.

**Safeway Baby Peeled Carrots**

# Ingredients:
# Carrots

## 9 Piece Super Bouncers
### (bouncing balls)

# This toy is a small ball.

Presumably that's bad.

**In-Sink-Erator Food Waste Disposer 444**

# Do not put fingers or hands into a waste disposer.

**Zep Upholstery Cleaner**

# Caution:
# Eye irritant.

**Window Blinds Cord Tag**

(unknown make)

# Warning:
## This device will not prevent strangulation hazard if young children wrap pull cords around their necks.

**Black Cat Black Snakes Fireworks**

# Caution
# flammable.
# Do not put
# in mouth.

# Note:
You can always
use Mineral Ice
as directed, but
its use is never
intended
to replace your
doctor's advice.

**Black Cat Race Car Firework**

# Caution:
# Moves on ground.
# Light fuse and
# get away.

**Basic Texture Get Curly
Curl Enhancing Shampoo**

# If any adverse reaction, discontinue use.

**Toll Booth Movable Arm**

# Caution:
# Moving arm
# can cause
# bodily injury.

## Mack's Ear Seals

# These earplugs ... may interfere with breathing if caught in the windpipe.

That's one way to keep things quiet.

**Vick's NyQuil**

# When using this product marked drowsiness may occur.

This product is a cold remedy to be taken at night to help you sleep.

## Tagamet HB200

# Do not use if you are allergic to Tagamet HB200 or other acid reducers.

The product is *named* Tagamet HB200— shouldn't that be enough of a clue to not use it if you know you are allergic?

**Gila Collapsable Window Shade**

# Caution:
# Remove shade
# before operating vehicle.

### Gold Dial

## Use Gold Dial as you would ordinary soap.

### Spring Water Dial

## Use Spring Water Dial as you would ordinary soap.

### Tropical Escape Dial

## Use Tropical Escape Dial as you would ordinary soap.

What would happen if you used any of these as *extraordinary* soap?

### Palm Beach Barbie Doll

# Dolls cannot
# stand alone.

Now there is a profound warning: Not!

**Band-Aid**

# For medical emergencies
# seek professional help.

**Bear Mace**

# May not work in all situations.

**Hormel Pepperoni**

# Do not eat packet.

Fraternities take note.

82

**Bowl Fresh Toilet Cleaner**

Safe to use around pets and children, although it is not recommended that either be permitted to drink from toilet.

**Bath & Body Works Linen Spray**

# For adult external use only. Avoid spraying in face or eyes.

**Mr. Bubbles Bath Bubbles**

# Not intended for human consumption.

**Bath & Body Works Moisture Rich
Body Lotion**

# Caution:
# This is not a toy.

We suppose some folks out there think rich
body lotion is a toy. Maybe in California.

**Cardinal Kids Collection Deluxe Marbles**

# Warning:
# Choking Hazard—
# this toy contains marbles.

**Estes Mini Super Shot Model Rocket Starter Set**

# This kit requires assembly.

**Black & Decker Hedge Hog 22"**
**Dual Action Hedge Trimmer**

# Danger:
# Risk of cut.

And don't run with scissors, either.

**Werner 10' Heavy Duty Ladder**

You should never
use a ladder if you
are not in good
physical condition.
Never walk,
bounce, or move
ladder while on it.

**Exide Ironclad Working Fork Lift**

# Do not lift personnel except on a securely attached platform.

**SpaTime pH Down**

# Never give anything by mouth to an unconscious person.

**Clorox Clean-Up Cleaner with Bleach**

# If vapors bother you, leave the room.

**Arm & Hammer Super Scoop Cat Litter**

# Note:
# Please wash hands
# thoroughly after
# handling *used*
# cat litter.

Our italics!

**WhirlOut Whirlpool Cleaner**

# Do not use
# while bathing.

Just when you thought it was safe

to go back into the spa.

**Coppertone SPF45 Sunblock**

# For external use only, not to be swallowed.

People must be afraid of sunburn in their mouths and throats.

Avoid long or quick
strides when walking
on surfaces with
questionable traction
such as wooden bridges,
steps, railroad ties, dead
grass, tile, hardwood
floors, or any other
terrain or surface which
may be either steeply
inclined, wet, hard,
or smooth.

**Equate Children's Allergy Elixir**

# When using this product: avoid alcoholic drinks, be careful when driving a motor vehicle or operating machinery.

"No, you can't take the car down to the liquor store, just sit down and watch 'Barney.'"

**Knight Kids Junior 7 Iron**

## Always make sure that no one is close enough to you to hit them.

Those junior golfers can get very competitive.

**7 UP**

# Point away from face and people, especially while opening.

**UC Berkeley Molecular Imaging Center**

# Do not look into laser with remaining good eye.

**Owner's Manual for a
1998 Volkswagen Golf and GTI**

If you have been
in an accident in
which the airbags
have deployed,
be sure to wash
your hands and
face with mild soap
and water
before eating.

**Bath & Body Works Peppermint Foot Spray**

# Caution:
# Avoid contact with face, eyes, and broken skin.

**Moose Mountain Toymakers—**
**Delicious Lookin' Fun Cookin' Play Food**

# Note to parents:
# We recommend
# washing all play food
# before using.

**Magnetic Power Alternative Pain Therapy**

# It does not provide a cure, nor make any medical claims.

What could possibly be medical about "Pain Therapy"?

**Crest Whitening Toothpaste**

# If you accidentally swallow more than used for brushing, get medical help or contact a poison control center right away.

Some people should stick to apples.

112

**SGI Iris Indigo Workstation**

# Don't dangle the mouse by its cable or throw the mouse at coworkers.

**Mr. Bubbles Body Wash for Kids of All Ages**

# Caution:
# Keep out of reach
# of young children.

**FungiCure Extra Strength**
(antifungal spray)

# Warning:
# Intended for use by normally healthy individuals only.

**Jackson, MS, Trade Mart**

# No soliciting allowed on trade floor

Aren't people *supposed* to solicit business
on a trade floor?

**Diflucan 150 mg tablet**
**(for yeast infection)**

# If overdose is suspected, contact your local poison control center or emergency room immediately.

The medicine comes in a bottle with one tablet in it.

**Little Ones Baby Lotion**

# Keep away from children.

**Rigdon Park Pool, Columbus, GA, in the "Play" Area**

# 0 feet 0 inches
# NO DIVING
# Too Shallow

Our hometown built three new "leisure pools" in the summer of 2002. We haven't lost anyone at the shallow end yet.

**Wal-Mart Sheriff Set**
(2 clicker guns with holsters, ammo belt
and sheriff's badge)

# Caution:
# Never point or
# shoot a gun at
# anyone.

Some would say it is also important to understand
the difference between a toy and the real thing.

**Hot Wheels Slingshotz Power Band Launcher**

# Warning:
# Do not point
# towards people
# or animals.

**Matchbox Rescue Net Motorized
Police SUV**

# Adults note:
# Cut the plastic
# attachments
# with scissors.

**Homemaker's Helper Handy Annie
Auto Fold One-Step Step Stool**

# Danger!
# Metal stools
# conduct
# electricity!

**Bansect Flea and Tick Collar for Cats**

# Do not allow children to play with collar.

**Stanley Heavy Duty GlueShot Glue Gun**

# Warning:
# Melted glue will
# burn skin.

**Enforcer 10-Minute Hair Clog Remover**

# Do not reuse empty container.

**Home Essentials 16" Oscillating Stand Fan**

# Never insert fingers through the Grille when Fan is running.

**Evenflo Position & Lock Plus Gate**

# Warning:
# This gate will
# not necessarily
# prevent
# all accidents.

Not even Spiderman can do that, right?

**Century Solara Stroller Model #6985**

# Warning:
# Never place child in the stroller with head towards the front of stroller.

Surely this was written by acrobatic parents.

**Hoover Upright Vacuum**

# Do not pick up anything that is burning or smoking, such as cigarettes, matches, or hot ashes.

**Bic Surestart Outdoor Lighter**

# Warning:
# Ignite lighter away from face and clothing.

**Hefty Clinch-Sak Tall Kitchen Bags**
(trash bags)

# Not recommended
# for food storage.

**Orange Clean Kitchen & Bathroom Wipes**

# Do not use for personal hygiene.

**Thermo Brand Vinyl Frame
Dreamspace Window Screens**

# Caution!!!
# Children can't fly.

Okay okay, we did it again. Despite extensive
research, we could *not* verify the warning rumored
to be on a super hero costume regarding flight.
We did track down this gem, however, which
implicitly advises parents that window screens
do not restrain children from falling out of
windows. The exclamation points are theirs.

**Sparkle Paper Towels**

# Caution:
# Improper microwave
# use can cause any
# paper product
# to burn.

**Pampers Bibsters**

# Choking may result from anything babies put in their mouths.

Obviously, a safe baby is a starved baby.

**Safety 1st Swivel Bath Seat**

# Warning:
# Prevent drowning.

**Nasco Paint Stripping Gloves**
(latex gloves)

# Warning:
# No glove resists
# all chemicals indefinitely.

**Conair Curling Iron**

# Caution—
# This product
# can burn eyes.

**Axius Glass Chalk**

# Warning:
# Do not block
# driver's vision.

Used car dealers can be very mischievous.

**Armor All Spray-on Car Polish
Protective Barrier**

# Disposal:
# Offer empty
# container for
# recycling.
# If recycling
# is not available,
# discard in trash.

And if there is no trash pickup?

**Amana Stainless Designer Series Washing Machine**

# For your safety: do not let children play in the washer.

And for the safety of the children?

**Monster Mask from Rubie's Costume Co.**

# Caution:
# A mask should
# never be worn as a safety
# helmet.

**Silica Gel**
(packet found in Dockers shoebox)

# Do not eat.
# Throw away.

In some circumstances it is okay to eat the shoes.

154

# Acknowledgments

We both would like to thank our families, who were always on the lookout for great warnings. Also, this book would not have been possible without the shelf-scouring skills of Miranda Floyd and Christine Rambo.

We would like to give special thanks to our former editor, Stephen Morrow, and the rest of the the staff at Simon and Schuster who put up with us as we settled into college life. Finally, we'd like to thank our new editor, Andrea Au, for helping to guide our project to completion.

# About the Authors

**Jeff Koon** graduated from high school in 2002 and currently attends the University of Georgia. He thought appearing on *The Montel Williams Show* with Andy in 2001 crowned his dot-com career—but then in the summer of 2002 they appeared on *20/20* and *Good Morning America* and things started really taking off. He lives in Georgia.

**Andy Powell** graduated from high school in 2002, having been voted "Most Likely to Succeed." After starting his first Web site with Jeff in high school, he was thrilled when their site listing stupid laws made Yahoo!'s site-of-the-year list in 1998. Currently attending the Georgia Institute of Technology as a National Merit Scholar, he lives in Georgia.

**Tim Carroll** is an illustrator and animator whose work has appeared in magazines, TV and Web sites in America, Japan, Germany, Hong Kong, Australia, and Iceland. He is a native San Franciscan.